THE SINCERE MILK

OF THE WORD

I Shall Not be Moved - A study of Fear

VOLUME 1

Clydestyle Publishing
4435 E. WT Harris Blvd
Charlotte, NC 28215
www.clydestyle.org

Ordering Information:
Quantity sales. Special discounts are available on quantity purchases by corporations, associations, and others. For details, contact the publisher at the address above.

ISBN-13: 978-0-578-17341-2

Printed in the United States of America

Dedication

In the loving memory of Jim Frank Miller for his love and devotion to the development of me.

Table of Content

Acknowledgements

I would like to take the time to thank everyone who had an encouraging word, lifted me up in prayer and supported me through this venture. I believe that God places people in your life for this cause and I am eternally grateful. I want to thank the Northside Church of Christ, particularly my fellow shepherds and all of the flock, as I had the pleasure of teaching them and watching lives change as the result of God's spoken word.

I want to thank the entire Mayberry family especially my parents, Annie and Leon, my siblings and my immediate household for the sacrifices they have made. I am thankful to be a Mayberry and proud of the rich tradition of talent we possess. I am thankful to all of my friends who have always been a source of encouragement and support. These particular friends I would like to mention because the depth of my studies and the sharpening of my spiritual sword came through my interactions with these men: Art Williams, Kate DoSoo, Anthony Gibson, Gary Culver, David Artist, Alan Young and a host of other men and women too numerous to name.

I was fortunate to have access to many books. I love to read and in addition to my formal schooling, I was blessed to find so many spiritual authors, too numerous to name, whose work touched my soul. I'm thankful to all bloggers, particularly on WordPress and the people who I have met all over the world on social media. I am grateful to all of my mentors and every person who thought to give me some words of wisdom.

Finally I want to thank my Lord and my God for every good and perfect gift produced in me. I pray that I may inspire and encourage others with my gifts and continue to let my light so shine that others would see my good work and glorify the Father in heaven. To Him be the glory! Amen!

Prologue

I am so grateful for the diversity of people I have met in my life. For they have helped me to keep an open mind for all people. I love people and my intent is to never alienate anyone. There will be a variety of people reading this book, some have met me and know me personally and then there are others who have never met me. There will be everything in between from the person who is acquainted with me and excited that I have written a book, to the critic who is thinking who does this guy think he is?

It is really hilarious to me because amongst all the various thoughts concerning this book, my heart's desire is to simply help someone. I do not believe that I am giving much opinion here. I believe that through my studies in the Word of God I have been led to this place. I believe that some of the things which I have experienced were divinely ordered. I was supposed to learn the things that I have learned, in the order I learned them and the way I learned them, so that I can pass it on.

This book is not meant to be a personal account per say as it is a spiritual journey with common sense application that has eternal benefits. I hope that is not vague. This is not a textbook, a dissertation for scholars or some exegetical discourse. These are the words of an unworthy guy, in an unlikely occasion, with the opportunity to magnify the Lord. If after reading this book you feel closer to God, then mission accomplished. If it causes you to evaluate some areas of your life where you have struggled, then I just hit a home run. And if it makes you smile, cry, shout and/or change for the better, then I present that as my evidence that God's hand guided this work.

This book is written for regular people who are searching. It is written for the person that has been made to feel less than. It is written for the person who occasionally experiences some suicidal ideation or just simply feels they are buckling from the weight of life. There is hope in this book. There are clear biblical principles presented here that should make your spiritual walk easier. You will feel that you understand your purpose in God's plan and how to go about executing that plan.

This particular book was six years in the making: Four years to understand and practice on myself and then two years of seeing it change lives through the people who had me as their life coach. I have dealt with grief, death, relationships, finances, job promotions, parenting and depression. In most of these cases I am coaching people who would not classify themselves as religious. Many could not put two scriptures together and make sense and although they were acquainted with Christ (basically had followed Mark 16:16), they had no depth or second teaching to learn how a life in Christ works. So, without being taught they began to do and learn God based on Hollywood's version. Movies taught them about God and fairytales were their application – and it was not working for them. So, instead of living this life like the child of the King they lived in fear – spiritual paupers left defenseless against their own vices.

What's worse is that religion and attending worship services just made them feel bad. Too many rules and regulations from a man-made playbook – and I'm not talking about creeds and the like, I am speaking of rules in God's kingdom which were not God's rules, but man's method of control. They were basically given their own modern-day set of Ten Commandments that worked against them. Things called new convert classes were designed to "teach you the ropes" and tell you what you cannot do and what you do not have scriptural backing for. Worship was taught as a thing to do instead of a way to be and what you learned on Sunday morning was not relevant to the conditions that daily wrestled against you.

Well, something had to be done. Although God is a spirit, clearly he gives us power in his word that we can feel. There is a "truthing" that needed to take place that even if you did not know what it was at the time, you knew how it made you feel. It is like the words reach your soul when you hear it. The words are both encouraging and inspiring at the same time. There is an inner joy that is activated when you hear these words and the fire of that joy burns forever. You begin to have confidence in what you hear from God. I mean you read his word with new life and anticipation. You once felt that God had forsaken you or worse you were too stupid to understand him and now you feel like his best friend.

What I am presenting in this book should not be treated like a new fad diet. I am telling you that this works for everyone because it came from the only person who created us and can save us. There is no gimmick – you will actually learn something that can never be taken from you. There will be feelings and negativity that will leave your life upon completion of this book. These works will breathe new life into you because they come from the book of life.

This book is not designed to take the place of you worshipping with like-minded believers. It is not to become your new vice or trump your reading of the scriptures. This book is to be shared. I would expect when you become enlightened you will let your light shine so that others can see it. I hope that when you become free, you will free others. It is my hope and prayer that this book will eliminate every reason you had to fear. God does not give us the spirit of fear, but of power, love and a sound mind (2 Tim. 1:7). I am going to show you how to live in that power.

Chapter I

The condition of the world could only be bad

In churches we sing a song that says this world is not my home, I'm just a passing through. It would be nice if we really took that statement to heart and allowed the world to do what it does and then not get caught up in it. Sight makes that very difficult. It is said that the eyes are the windows to the soul, but I think they are the bifocals to our lust. We want what we see and we live in a society that tells us we deserve it. We struggle with living life because somewhere along the way we were promised stuff. All kinds of stuff: White house with a picket fence; love and happiness; 40 acres and a mule; a rose garden and an opportunity. We were told to pull ourselves up by our bootstraps and hard work would pay off. Our Statue of Liberty is very welcoming to strangers, but if old Liberty could speak based on the things she has seen, she would definitely paint a different story about America and the world in general.

She would have mentioned the poor treatment of slaves and immigrants who came into this country. She would have seen the start, finish and results of all our lies regarding immigration. She would have seen the coming of the street pharmaceutical industry that would poison our nation and she would really know who was behind 9/11.

Biblically, it has been explained that sin entered the world through our first parents – and death followed shortly after that. There, the war between darkness and light was enhanced. You see that war was fought long before man and woman were created and in God's time it will end. So we can call it light and dark, obedience and disobedience, good and evil or spirit and carnal – but whatever the label the results are the same: Two sides will be presented to us and we have to choose.

This world was never supposed to be good. This was a test to see the effects of God's goodness on free-will bearing creatures, who could understand and make a decision. This world is the only glimpse of hell we get. The decay of the conscience and the mis-education of the creation, are the strengths of this place. And there are people choosing it every day. The news media provides the lens and the world is the stage, with 24 hour access viewing. People who are hurting show up to hurt other people and we watch and form unrighteous opinions about it. We run the gamut of emotions as we watch and it's difficult for us not to watch. Our society is evil to the point that even the good things are not worth mentioning. There is more than enough evidence against our big blue marble for us to lose the notion of this being our final resting place. Trust in the world will hurt you so bad. You have probably already experienced some of the pain I am talking about. We are hoping for perfection in an imperfect and hopeless place. We keep expecting more and being hurt because there is no "more". We keep expectations on all the nouns – people, places, things and even ideas – and we are let down. We expect our employers, government, churches and the like to produce and provide for our posterity and welfare and they all let us down.

As a result of being let down and expectations not met, some in our society turn to destruction of people and property. Mass shootings, rape, brutality, uncontrolled anger, theft, extortion, lies and racism are just a few of the world's favorite vices. When our biases run out of control, these vices are enhanced. One of the first lessons you will learn about God and the world is that the attitude and response to things are different – almost opposite. If the world does something you can almost bet the farm that God's way would be the opposite. The world's solution to hatred is more hate, with the logic that in a contest of hate, you have to hate more to win. And the hate is justified because the other side hates too. God's solution to hate is love. Unconditional love is one of the strongest tools in the spiritual arsenal to fight hate. And hate cannot almost beat love – the fight is not even close.

Take acceptance for example: Our world has an acceptance problem. Many of our troubles and struggles come from our inability to accept one another. So, in our initial relationship with our heavenly Father, we were separated from the commonwealth of God by our sins. It is impossible for us to be accepted by God on our own. Despite many failed attempts over thousands of years, we only proved that we are sinners and lost forever in darkness.

Then, Jesus comes and dies for the sins of the world so that we have the opportunity to be "accepted in the beloved." Now empowered by the Holy Spirit, we who believe live to bring this joyous occasion of salvation to others. Acceptance not only says that you belong, but it also says that you belong just the way you are. Acceptance is the bridge that allows the sinner in darkness to fellowship with the light. Without acceptance a connection cannot be made. And it's in that fellowship that the magic happens. The apostle John wrote that if we walk in the light as he is in the light, we have fellowship one with another and the blood of Jesus Christ his son cleanses us from all sin – that's a pretty powerful fellowship! But if I am not accepting, it's all for naught!

Have you ever felt like you did not belong? Have you ever been in a situation where others have made you to feel that way? It's a horrible feeling, but do you know we do that whenever we decide that another person does not matter. You do not have to conform to the way I think for me to accept you. You don't have to look like me, live like me or eat the same things I do for me to accept you. I accept you because I have been accepted. The thought of me cheapening my acceptance or taking it for granted because I don't accept you, is not an option for me. My acceptance of you is my judgment of you and as for me and my house, we choose to accept.

This is really about living in the world, but not being like the world. This comes down to my ability to be changed or conformed into the image of Christ. This thought will be further developed in another chapter. I still marvel at God's eyes...he looks at us differently. God sees us for who we can become. So because of my understanding of how God looks at me, I should look at others the same way.

Have you ever wondered how he does that? I mean how does the creator of the universe look past our faults? Do you think it bothers him to see us as a fallen creature? Do you think he gets tired of taking the high road and suffering certain things to be so in order to bring about his end? When God said he "so loved" the world. He really meant it!

The bible tells us that it was while we were yet sinners; Christ died (Rom. 5:8). That means that in the midst of our sins and at our weakest point, we deserved death, but God sent his son to die instead. When God created "justice" he knew what he was doing. God would not allow justice to be violated by his love for us. Justice demanded death to the guilty and our God satisfied both – Justice got its death, we got our salvation and grace and mercy was born.

Because of this, the New Testament writers remind us of what God did as a method of encouraging us to return the favor. God expects our appreciation for what he has done to show in our actions towards one another. God wants us to look beyond someone's faults and not only see them for what they can become, but start treating and helping them reach that potential.

It's easy to hold grudges, keep records of wrongdoings and alienate someone from your life, but it is the true worshipper who has the eyes of God. This, my friend, is the beauty of being in Christ. We are early on this journey but I want you to understand that the covenant relationship that belongs to us is not only approved of by God but he is the guarantor of it.

Children are a great example of this because they are so easy to please. As my children progress into their late teens I reflect back on how easy it has been to care for them. All things considered, I've been able to provide their needs and most of their wants. I can say to them do not worry about this or that because I would take care of whatever they feared. They live under the safe covering of dad! There are things and situations that they could not even imagine having to experience. In fact many of the horrors of this life are locked away forever in the "make believe" section of their minds because they would swear today that it could not happen to them in "real life".

I know of and have counseled kids who came home from school and all of their favorite things were laying in the yard being picked over by their neighbors. I have listened to children lament about being caught in the middle of a boxing match between their parents and me trying to explain fear away from them because they witnessed such anger. A daughter now believing her father is capable of such rage that if he could beat her mom unconscious, it's only a matter of time before she has her turn.

From jail to drugs to violence and sex, kids of all ages have had to deal with these things far too soon. As men we have the responsibility when raising a family to make sure certain evils are kept out of the house and God's goodness is freely flowing within. There is a sacred trust we hold as dads to be the guarantor of good things.

This role should not be taken lightly because you see when we do it correctly we imitate a character of God that the rest of the family will believe and trust in for the rest of their lives. If I am the guarantor of good things for my family, and they know and understand that the source of my guarantee is the Almighty himself, then when it is time to turn them over to our father in heaven, that task is made simple. They will already have a love and fondness for the heavenly father because they are very comfortable with the works of the earthly father. More importantly they learn how to return gratitude for goodness.

God among other things is my guarantor. All of his promises are backed by his personal guarantee that nothing is too difficult, too powerful or too challenging for him. God loves spending time demonstrating this fact to his followers. As feeble little children we reach up to the father with all of our fears and anxiety and he reaches down smiling and picks us up. I really love that imagery! So when I start to think about the goodness of God and the recklessness of the world, I am very happy that I chose him. The world was never meant to be good.

Chapter 2

Decisions and challenges

Well now that we have the condition of the world out of the way we can move on to the meat of the matter. The greatest question particularly when we talk religion is why are there so many? There are so many religions and so few explanations and there are people participating in religions they do not understand. To make matters worse, when trouble comes, you find out the hard way that there is no relevant understanding of scripture to rest the mind. We have challenges and we need to make some decisions!

Many are still in their parent's religion and sadly the same preacher or pastor is still there. That religion being a journey would be the last thing to call it as stagnant growth, death and complacency has been the norm. It is a struggle and a chore just to get up and go to the church building where you already know what will happen because it happens that way repeatedly. Brother so and so will say that usually long prayer, and speak it in the King James English. Same sister will cry, same brother will shout and the same people will be late. Giving will be over emphasized and liturgy will have more control than Jesus. Our worship is staged instead of a spontaneous response to the love God has shown us.

We endure this because we are told it is right – that somehow this is what God wanted. Why in the world would God want us to be disinterested and on autopilot when it comes to worshipping him? Is there something wrong with us? Are we the only ones that feel this way? This confusion lasts a lifetime and then on our deathbeds is the only time we question and wonder if what we did was the right thing; and what we said was the right stuff; and what we obeyed was the right command. These are the things that make religion so difficult. This is the core of our fear – that what we do not understand will lead to our eternal demise.

I am not trying to belittle anyone's religion or beliefs. I just want to bring to your conscience an awakening. I believe ultimately that if your heart is sincere and you really want to be pleasing to God, then he will show you the way – no matter where you are spiritually today.

Most of us can relate to the story of the Ethiopian Eunuch found in the book of Acts chapter 8 and verses 28-39. This is a beautiful account of the salvation received by this man who had a heart toward God. This Eunuch was even trying to worship God as the text says he had travelled to Jerusalem with that purpose in mind.

So he's reading the scriptures with not much understanding so we know he was not a scholar in this field. He was an educated man most likely and he was entrusted to oversee Queen Candace's wealth. I love the fact that this Eunuch having much money and power still chose to acknowledge God. This is my evidence that if you have a sincere desire to please God, he will show you the way.

Philip, God's servant, finds this Eunuch's chariot in the desert and they begin to have a conversation. Philip asks about his understanding of what he was reading and this rich fellow was smart enough to know that he needed a guide for that – we all do. The conversation centered on an Old Testament passage – Isaiah 53 – and the Eunuch could not understand whether the prophet Isaiah was talking about himself in the text or someone else. It turns out he was talking about someone else.

Philip began at the same scripture and taught Jesus to the Eunuch. To just say he taught Jesus to him is such a broad stroke. There is a lot to talk about when you engage the subject of Jesus. Undoubtedly, this was not a debate between two men who had conflicting religious views. Nor was this a case of a stronger man belittling or trying to control a weaker man. This was a case of one spiritual man attempting to glorify God by teaching another man who was trying to glorify God. They were at two different spiritual stages of the same journey – to honor their creator! The Spirit brought them together and the same scenario and result has been playing out the same way for centuries.

Philip teaches Jesus and when the Eunuch sees water it triggers an urgent response. God's word should always have this effect on us. There are various circumstances in life that demand our immediate response, should not a response to God be first? After being taught about Jesus, the Eunuch saw water and asked what was hindering him from being baptized? If we learn nothing else from this text we should learn that you cannot teach Jesus without teaching baptism. The Eunuch allowed the word of Christ in his heart and demonstrated his obedience to that word by surrendering his life to a watery grave and resurrecting from that grave a new creature created in Christ Jesus for the purpose of doing good work. This is our first spiritual act designed to eliminate our fear because we receive a powerful new name after this process that the unseen world will recognize and fear.

Salvation puts us in a covenant relationship with God the Father and this all started by us making the right decision in our response to him. If there is a God working on my behalf, then why would I be afraid? We live in a world that gives us many things to fear. Fear is relative. My fears may not be your fears but we cannot deny fear especially when our body naturally starts to process it. We all have an almond-shaped mass of grey matter inside each cerebral hemisphere which is involved with the experiencing of emotion (amygdala) and when it perceives danger, our pheromone molecules start transmitting and our bodies go into fear mode. The fight or flight gland gets summoned and we get active. The truth is that it doesn't take much for us to fear. Even when we do not know nor understand the imminent danger, our brains just make up the parts we do not know. Fear is like our imaginations playing "make believe" with reality.

For God hath not given us the spirit of fear; but of power, and of love, and of a sound mind. I really believe this, but clearly in our society people are afraid. The fear clouds our judgement and makes it difficult for us to negotiate sound decisions. Life was never designed for God's elect to live in fear. There are things he has done for us mentally, spiritually, emotionally and physically so that we would not fear. We need to choose to trust God instead.

The 23rd psalm is all about eliminating fear from the mind of the child of God. It was written for us to remember the state in which the Lord, our shepherd, has left us. If we believe that the Lord is really our shepherd and we won't be lacking in anything as the first verse says, then it's easy to see that the first four things God does, should take away all of our reasons to fear.

The text says "he makes", "he leads", "he restores" and "he leads" again. All that hard work goes to waste if we receive it and still fear. The "still waters" and the "green pastures" speak to our physical needs. The "paths of righteousness" speaks to our spiritual being and I'm sure you need no help with what "restoration" speaks too as it reaches our very souls.

Then the text declares that evil would not be feared because God is with us. And not only is he with us, but his "rod" (discipline) and "staff" (authority) comfort us. The structure of the writing of this Psalm is interesting to note. In a literary sense, the delayed identification of the true intent of this psalm leads us to believe that it is about just God's provisions for us. But right in the middle of the psalm is this statement about fear.

You see, we fear because we cannot control everything. And we only need control because of our wants and desires. I want my family to be safe, I want to provide for them, I want to live to see my grandchildren and I want to make it home safe tonight. The truth is I do not control any of the things.

These things are only hopes and dreams that information or lack of information will cause panic. As much as I desire it, I cannot guarantee the safety of my family even if they were with me 24/7 and we were all armed. I want to provide for my family but in 21 years I have been fired or laid off five times. I want to see my grandkids but I do not control the time I have left here. And making it home safe is not up to me either. As we drive the highways we are challenged by torpedo-like objects zooming towards us. I have no control over who is driving the other vehicles nor do I have control over road conditions or mechanical malfunctions with my vehicle. So when any of these things are challenged – meaning something happens to cloud the future so I cannot see the outcome – I get scared. Well this is the part where we are to rely on our shepherd who said we would not be in want.

However, want in the text does not mean that if I want a new car then he will not let me stay in want, he will just get me a new car – oh how we all wish it worked that way. In the text, "want" means lacking so he really promised that we would always be in a place to receive what we need. Now, whether we do the things to get what we need is questionable. This concept teaches us something very profound about God. It's a characteristic about him that we tend to forget – God is the quintessential teacher! What I mean is, other than it being our time to depart this world; all other things are for our learning. We are in a constant state of learning and in a lifetime we will never stop learning. Science has proven that our brains can do a lot of things and it pretty much never shuts off.

Its complexities have still baffled scientists to this day, but they all agree that for something that represents three percent of the body's weight and uses 20 percent of the body's energy, the brain is pretty fascinating.

So our God is always teaching us and increasing our faith. He wants to see us conform into the image and character of his son. So to get us there we endure trials – many that we have brought upon ourselves, but all these things our God allows for the purpose of eliminating fear from our bodies. God's plan is for us to understand what is going on and make decisions that will glorify him – fear hinders this plan and so it must be neutralized.

So dear reader, are you ready to lay aside the cares of this world that so easily stifle us and receive the word of the Lord which is able to save your soul? Your decision is your response and if you are really ready to embrace this life changing information I have written in these pages, then let's pray together for clarity and read on!

Chapter 3

Putting the Good News back in the Gospel

So the journey begins with understanding that years of religious wars have dirtied up the Gospel of Christ. Not that the effects or facts have changed just the way the gospel is carried. Those who are supposed to carry or bring the gospel to the world sometimes get caught up in worldly things that they allow that to distort the message.

I was counseling a woman whose mother always told her from a preteen up that sex was dirty and nasty and it hurt and she probably wouldn't like it. This mother had very good intentions and what she was trying to express to

her daughter was the good message
that sex is something God created to be
perfected in Holy Matrimony and
when the time comes the young lady
would have a male caller who would
want to get to know her permanently.
They would marry and after that, have
the free will to enjoy all the pleasures
of marriage and working together with
a life partner.

The message did not quite come out
like that, in fact it is so skewed that it
is a totally different message. One
message speaks of something
wonderful to hope for and the other
speaks of something to worry about.
How is this possible when we are
talking about the same message?

The gospel has been done the same
way. Some will tell you the gospel
from the negative: Once you become a
Christian you can't do this or that

anymore and you better do such and such and life as you know it must change. Some make the gospel sound like life stops after the conversion! Some preach Christ with so many rules and regulations that it makes the beauty and clear attraction to the gospel difficult to see.

In the first century Paul dealt with this issue and said to the church at Philippi to beware of dogs, evil doers and mutilators of the body. He was well aware of the foolishness that would come from the Jews particularly when it came to the gentiles and how they were to receive Christ.

The Jews were attempting to create another Gospel by adding that gentiles must be physically circumcised, and would always be second class citizens of the Kingdom because they did not have the lineage back to Abraham.

Christ's gospel was always intended to be inclusive to everyone who would call on the name of the Lord. This was a "whosoever will" gospel that welcomed the sincere heart that understood its undone condition and wanted to be made whole God's way.

The word Gospel means good news and we need to be careful not to hinder that meaning. Is the gospel still good news for the world today? Absolutely! And this writer assumes you have responded to the gospel so all I want to do is remind you of what the gospel means, to encourage you to honor God in it.

In Romans the eighth chapter, the writer speaks of a wonderful position where in the child of God has been placed. This is the conclusion of several points the apostle Paul was making beginning in Romans the fifth chapter. I am trying not to get too complicated, but what he says in chapter eight should excite you forever! In the first verse – as I paraphrase his statement – Paul says that if you are in Christ and you are walking after the spirit, then you have no punishment. Literally he is saying that there is no fault charged to you if you are in Christ. Now this statement does not mean that you should exercise your right to sin because grace has you covered. What it does mean is that since you were born again, you are now dead to sin and you do not live anymore in it. Now what I did not say is that in this life you must be perfect. Jesus was perfect for you. You must be faithful and that is God's expectation for you. He even put in this wonderful plan a way for you to correct the times when you are not faithful. And as long as you are practicing these things, you are walking in the Spirit and there is no punishment waiting for you.

I know right?!?! Exciting stuff, but let me say it another way to try and make it more clear. God had a plan before the foundation of the world that he would save mankind. Now we know all of mankind will not be saved because all of mankind will not chose salvation. For those that do, God himself has satisfied the punishment of sin in Christ Jesus, he has created a provision for you to have life more abundantly through his son, and he has provided a way for you to be cleansed when you get dirty.

So, I am saying that the death of Jesus Christ reconciled you back to God and the life of Jesus Christ saves you (Rom. 5:10). All you have to do is live by faith in the son of God who loved you and gave himself for you!

This is powerful stuff and I want you to understand it in its purest form.

There are some who would trouble you with this information because they do not think you can handle it. This is where they would also attempt to emphasize your faith pattern and faith tradition as equally important to your salvation. These are separate items. They think you may start taking your liberties in Christ for granted and become misguided in your thoughts thinking that somehow you could fool God in regards to matters of the heart. Of course we know that this is impossible and we need to be more responsible with the information. There should not, in addition to what God wants, be another set of man-made rules to work against you. Our God did not leave room for man to give a thought or opinion on how we were to be saved.

So this exciting news is only part of it. To know what God has done on our behalf is awesome, but how he did it is even more spectacular. From verse number one of Romans eight we drop down to verses 29 and 30. There are five things I need to explain as God's process for redeeming us. The text says that God foreknew us. His foreknowledge means a few things for us. It means that we cannot surprise God with our sin, in fact he knew every single decision we would make before we made it. Then the text says that those he foreknew, he predestined. The combination of the two things is powerful on our behalf.

Foreknowledge means he knows and predestined means he put us on a plan. God put us on a plan based on what he knew of us. We are not all on the same plan, but the same God who knows the number of hairs on our

head, put us on a plan based on what
he knew of us individually. He knew
the good, bad and ugly decisions. He
knew the sins and every vice that trips
us. He knew all of our choices – good
and bad – and created a plan for us that
would change us to be like his son.
This is a plan, my friends, which we
cannot mess up with our foolishness!
My sins cannot trump God's plan no
more than it can trump the blood of
Christ. I can freely walk away from
God's plan, but as long as my heart is
soft toward God and I live a life trying
to put him first, then there is no way
this plan does not work – unless again
you decide to walk away from God.
Anyone willing to stay will reach
God's end.

If that was not enough our God,
upon our demonstration of faith, knew
us and used what he knew to create a
plan and then the text says he called

us. Not like a telephone type call, but it means to give us a new name so that the world would know who we belonged to and that name was Christian. The word simply means that we are "of" or "belonging to" Christ.

The fourth thing he did after knowing us, putting us on our own plan and giving us a new name, is he justified us which means he transferred Christ's righteousness to us and transferred our foolishness and sin to Christ. Of course you know he took our sin and foolishness and nailed it to the cross. This is incredible news that we do not deserve. This alone is the reason that I want to serve the Lord and completely surrender to him.

The plan would not be complete without that last item which is that he glorified us. For God to glorify us means that he sees us whole or complete. He sees us as the completed version and not the struggling version. He sees us in triumph and not tragedy.

I call this the cake theory. The cake theory goes this way: If you were at home making a cake and you mixed the batter just right and put it in the oven, no one would proclaim that they have put cake batter in the oven. Everyone would say they have cake in the oven. And we would be anticipating the cake and preparing for it. We would make ready for the arrival of the cake and once it is in the oven, no one thinks of it as cake batter anymore. So is with our God and us: He sees us at his end and not in some stumbling sin on a mission he cannot complete. For this cause, we are crucified with Christ, nevertheless we live, yet not us, but Christ lives in us. Now *ain't* that good news!

Chapter 4

My lifestyle is not meant to be accompanied by fear

So God gave us all one life and that was for the purpose of us growing and developing into a state where we would function in our right minds, and make decisions for our wellbeing.

There are so many things in this world to get us off this task. This world is all about influence and control. We fight each day to keep our righteous minds. Look at your life and the forces around you. Your home life, your job, your friends, the products you buy, the services that you use, everywhere you turn someone is trying to get you to do something. Buy this thing, support that cause, help him out – there is no end.

From the time you wake up and even in your sleep, life is getting away from you. The status quo gives you a license to do almost anything. Its motto is simple: Do unto others before they can do to you.

So you my friend must take control of your own self. We don't often consider it but for many the word "sale" means you need to buy and you would be crazy to let this deal go. Did you need the item? It doesn't matter because it's on sale. For some, hearing the words happy hour means it's time to drink. Why, are you thirsty? No, it's happy hour and I must take advantage of this deal.

Look at the control these simple words have on us. Our words have the same effect as controlled substances – and we are hooked. So how is this fixed? We must take control of our own lives. Life was meant to be led. You have to get out in front of your life and lead it. Guide it. Control it. Treat it as precious as it is. Critical thinking is paramount to your success. Make no mistake: this isn't about just surviving, it's all about flourishing.

So how do we flourish? Great question! In the epistle written to the Philippians the apostle Paul who lived a good portion of his life as Saul of Tarsus and had quite the credentials, spoke of this. He saying that his accolades are no longer important to him because the Excellency of Christ is a far greater covet. Once he learned of the goodness of God and his wonderful plan for our lives and the benefits we have in Christ Jesus, anything Paul could accomplish on his own does not even matter anymore. What a way to be! To not be driven by your own gain, but to have an accelerated push for the Excellency of Christ is powerful.

So what is this accelerated push? Paul gives us three things: The first is that we would *know* him. The first push Paul says is that there is something beneficial about intimately knowing Christ, and sadly too many of us have not grown past the acquaintance stage. To know Christ is to be free and this freedom allows us to drop insignificant things from our lives, thereby focusing on the weightier matters such as hungering and thirsting after righteousness. Just getting to know Jesus intimately helps you do that. There are specific characteristics about Jesus that you need to know. Jesus never worried about gossip. He never bothered with "he said, she said" stuff. Jesus made good use of his time and did not take it for granted. All of his life people plotted against him, challenged him, cursed him, and hated him. He could have responded in a million different ways of revenge, but he did not. He simply committed himself to God. God is the one who judges righteously and Jesus committed himself to his Father in heaven (1 Pet. 2:23). In other words, Jesus suffered things because of his faith in God. His faith kept him focused, steadfast and unmovable despite his circumstance. If I get to know him, I will be that way too. Knowing Christ constitutes that I would have an attitude change. If I was known as an angry person before Christ, I cannot afford to carry that anger over. I must surrender. Now my friend, place your struggles upon his shoulders, and leave it, just simply because you have come to know Christ intimately.

The second thing is the power of his resurrection. I wish that we as the body of Christ understood this principle better. When we get down, we are down and out. We have pity parties, we act as though God has forsaken us and we even forget who we belong to. In theory we understand that trouble will come to us and that God promised to never leave us nor forsake us, but . . . We still act like God did not say that. The power of his resurrection is a principle that we benefit from today, but we do not use it.

The power of the resurrection is given to us not only to be used on Judgment Day when we rise, but also for the trials of life. What I am saying is that when we stumble and fall, God has already given us what we need to get up. I have the power to rise out of my afflictions. I have been empowered by God during my fall, the power to elevate. The scriptures explain it this way: "I can do all things through Christ which strengthens me."

Sometimes we pray for things that God has already provided. The power of his resurrection is available to us today. When I stumble and fall, I'm living in the power of his resurrection which means that there is nothing that happens to me that will be too much to bear. Even in death, as a child of God, what do you think will happen to me if my "fall" is death? When I was baptized I came out of that water by faith to walk in a new life. A life created in Christ Jesus, by the father, that would be a good work. Therefore, I was baptized and rose with power. When I die, the bible says I will have a resurrection like his (Rom. 6:5).

So then if the beginning of my life in Christ and the end both contain a resurrection, why does my life have to differ? I contend that when we go through our trials and tribulations God has made us more than conquers. When I fall, he has given me the power to get up. The only reason we think we cannot get up is a lack of faith. There is power in falling if I don't deny it. When Jesus went down, he did not have the power he had when he got up. Therefore there is power in the fall. God designed it that way so that we can bear witness of his resurrection. I will bear that witness at my spiritual birth, my death and every day in between. If my example, Christ, did it, then how can this not be the case for me?

The third thing is the fellowship of his suffering. If I know him and share in the power of his resurrection then how can I not want to take part in this fellowship? This is the part that attaches me to the body of Christ. This does not refer to his suffering on the cross. I could not have taken that and I am not worthy to take that – he is the perfect sacrifice, not me. I am worthy to share in the suffering of his body – the body of Christ i.e. the people.

The body of Christ is something I am a part of and just as if I stubbed my toe and the rest of my body would respond, so is the way I must be as a part of the body of Christ. I am a part of the body and my proof of that is how I respond to the needs of that body. I am called to be an active member of the body of Christ, not a dead member. So all of the graces given to us in this body are designed for us to be partakers of the same grace. There is a song we often sing: "I will work, I will pray and I will labor

everyday in the vineyard of the Lord."
The vineyard is the body of Christ. So
this song is about helping the church,
not spreading the gospel. We need to
do both, but let us not forsake the
church. Let us be an active part of the
suffering for this is the purpose of our
lives. So as a part of our fellowship,
you need food and I have a house full
of food. Is there really a need to pray
to the father about this? He has already
provided. The issue will be how will I
deal with my covetousness?
Or what about a family that is left
homeless because of layoffs and plant
closings? Is this a matter for the
government or the church? If this
family is on the fold, it is a matter of
the church. I am not saying that we
should not help people who need
Jesus. I am saying that I need to give
emphasis and preference to the
household of faith (Gal. 6:10).

In Christ we share in the suffering of the body. No one goes through trials alone. If we follow God's plan, our fellowship was set up for this purpose which is why Jesus said, " ...by this will all men know that you are my disciples if you have love one for another."

Chapter 5

My spiritual family

At the close of the last chapter we talked about the body of Christ. In this chapter I want to attempt to explain to you the complexities of the family of God. It is only hard to understand because our eyes deceive us. Our vision helps to create biases and expectations. Our carnality leads us to place our focus upon what is not instead of what really is. We suffer from not practicing what we preach, being judgmental and unforgiving. The modern day church has found itself in probably the worst state in which it has ever been.

I am going to paint a picture of how God sees the church which is in direct contrast with how we see it and how we treat it. I want to show it to you from the perfect lens of scripture and then encourage you, dear reader, not to be discouraged by what you see, but to become a partaker in this new understanding to the glory of God.

So we know that the church is the body of Christ and the kingdom of Christ here on earth. He reigns supreme in this gathering of believers, though some might call it cult-like, due to the unfeigned faith each member has for the king. And throughout the New Testament one can find many examples of how the body of Christ functions and relates to Christ, its head. And from that vantage point it becomes even easier to see how the relationship with the head affects the horizontal relationships throughout the membership, one to another, as well as with the world. So, ideas like service, forgiveness, unconditional love, faithfulness, compassion, truth and longsuffering should always abound within the body. When it is done right, there is a definite unified fellowship and sense of having all things common among the believers. Judgement has no place here, only encouragement to be the best that you can be and loving support when you stumble.

A placebo is a measure designed merely to calm, please or pacify another. It is more for a psychological benefit than for any spiritual effect. There can also be a placebo church, which only exists as a method to control. It is only a form of godliness, but it denies the power thereof. This would be the opposite of the Lord's church. In the Old Testament we see how God made many attempts to allow Israel to be his people and sin kept getting in the way. We read about the

longsuffering of God and understand
his love for mankind in sending his son
to take away the sins of the world. And
he protected his seed through the
generations and fulfilled all prophecy
which became the greatest evidence
that he was truly God.

The father in heaven is very serious
about his family. Like any good father
he wants his family to enjoy what he
provides and because of his goodness,
treat one another with love and respect.
One of the great things about love and
respect is that it is contagious. So
imagine being at a church where love
and respect is only an idea. It normally
means that no one is practicing this
concept, or they were practicing and
they got discouraged before it caught
on. This means that all new Christians
that come into this love-less and
respect-less fold simply need to not get
caught up in the discouragement, but

spread the love. Part of the mission of the church – second to saving souls – is sharing the love we experience unconditionally. Your mission, if you choose to accept it, is to spread love and respect in the environment where you dwell. Despite how it looks, the world desperately needs more examples of love and respect. Are you up for the challenge?

Chapter 6

Unconditional Love

The abstract has much more depth than the concrete. Yet the only reason that we covet the concrete is because we can see it. We negate the running of our imaginations and the creativity stimulated by the abstract all for a neat little bundle produced by the concrete. It is the difference in reading a book and watching a movie – our problem is that in our society we have a whole lot more moviegoers.

When the medium of television was created it was the latest technology and designed to open our creativity in a visual way. Now there could be much more learning taking place because our eyes and ears can work together to collect data instead of audio only, as it was with radio. Still today we have the history channel, discovery channel, and even a science channel – and they do have a viewership – but these channels cannot compete with TNT, ESPN, TBS or even OWN. Today, 90 percent of what is on TV does not stimulate our brains to think or grow. TV is mostly for entertainment – a boob tube to hold you hostage so that you can be bombarded with advertisements.

What's worse is that what we see will be destroyed. So why do we covet what we see? We even take beautiful abstract concepts and ruin them by placing the focus on the object of the abstract and not the concept. Let me make this simpler: Some people will love (abstract concept) a person and place the thrust or emphasis of their love on the person, instead of the concept of love, itself. So God gives us unconditional love to use here on earth. Another person's behavior does not cancel unconditional love. Circumstances and situations should prove the unconditional effects of love, but instead we allow situations and circumstances to control our demonstration of love. For instance, when a relationship ends or the person being loved does not measure up to the expectations of the one loving, the relationship ends and the person loving says I'm not going to love anymore. Or say two people are madly in love and one dies. The one still alive chooses not to get involved in a love relationship anymore because it's too painful.

You see, love is not the source of the pain or anger in either case. Failed expectations and grief, respectively, are the culprits in those cases, but love was blamed. Love never changed in either case. Love can still be developed and should still be resolute. It should be locked and loaded for the next episode, not tossed aside like a smoking gun that killed the relationship. So if we kept this in perspective – we should keep love pure. It was never meant to be conditional. It was never meant for profit and it should never be associated with negative acts. Love is an everlasting stream of God in you. It will never do you any harm and will save you from a lot of hurt.

So love should be as it is taught in scripture: We are to love one another because love is of God and he who loves is born of God and knows God. On the contrary, he who does not love does not know God; for God is love. This seems like such a hard line. If you don't love it doesn't say that you are not acting like God. It says you do not even know him. And the reason is clear: If God is love and you act like you don't know how to love then, I guess you don't know love or God. Ouch!

So as a child, I first learned love from my mother. She constantly did things for me. She even anticipated a whole lot of things on my behalf. I remember when I was a child I got fevers often and she was off to the races to get me to the ER in the middle of the night. She is my everything. Now, of course, my dad was there providing for the household but it's not until later in life that you understand those sacrifices. So both parents raised me up in an environment that was beneficial to me. My surroundings were important to my emotional stability and it enhanced my physical, spiritual and mental development.

So I was acquainted with God's love, but I did not understand it. I enjoyed the way my parents expressed their love for me but I thought it was just how they were or maybe even they were obligated. Their love for me came full circle when I fathered my own children. Along the way I learned about God being the source of love and how this love could cover a ton of sin. I still did not know how, but I had read the sacred text. My children gave no added value to our relationship as I gave no value to my parents, but as parents we practice the love of God in us and the objects of our love reap the benefits.

So now the love we get from God is supposed to be the catalyst for the love we give. In other words, because of God's love, we love – just like God. Unconditional love is bottled at the source which is God. And anyone drinking from this spring will produce the same. So, my parents first loved me and then I loved my kids and since I first loved them, they will love their children and so on. Never is the object of love supposed to be the originator. My parents loved because God first loved them and they passed down that love through the generations.

Love is never an even exchange. It cannot be measured and it will never be as strong as the original source – which is God. Love is an action that is designed to move, support, enhance and embody life. It is greater than a feeling, larger and stronger than fear and more powerful than anything else in the world. It cannot be purchased, bartered or stolen. The Holy writ says love bears all things, believes all things, hopes all things and endures all things and it never fails.

Now this is just a glimpse of love, but too much that isn't love, has been called love. Sadly, many have mistaken love for something hurtful or even deadly. Love has been used to mask hidden agendas and fool the minds of the simple. Love has taken the blame for results and conclusions which should never have been associated with this beautiful concept. A man says he loves his wife only to catch her in bed with another man and he kills them both – love crime? I think not. Another man claims to be in love with a woman who is not friendly to his advances. He eventually rapes her – because of love? Ha! God forbid!

To truly understand love you must process it with the spiritual heart. I learned the concept of the spiritual heart from one of my professors during the course of earning my masters. This concept forever changed how I understood relationships and how information is to be processed. You cannot understand or administer unconditional love without it. There are four parts to the heart – which is not really the organ that pumps blood, but the mind. Sometimes in scripture the bible subscribes the ability of thought to the heart. The organ that pumps blood cannot think. There is only one organ doing that and it would be the mind.

So for example Romans 6:17 says, "But God be thanked, that ye were the servants of sin, but ye have obeyed from the heart that form of doctrine which was delivered you." Is it possible to obey from an organ designed to pump blood? Of course not, it would be possible if the "obey" was from the mind – which is the case here. So when I say the spiritual heart I am really talking about your mind.

As I said earlier there are four parts to the heart. The first part is the intellect. This is the filter in which all information is to be processed. All data that comes our way must go first through the intellect filter. This is for the purpose of using one of the greatest tools God gave man. When we were made in His image it was not that we would "look like" God but that we would share the trait of intellect. God knows and because he knows, we know. We are able to process information and make decisions based on what we think. Animals instinctively do things which are contrary to our way of brain function and utilization.

Once information is processed through our intellect, it is stored in our conscience for later use. If we have processed correctly then the conscience becomes our most powerful tool to keep us unspotted from this present world. If we have processed incorrectly, then the conscience does us no good. You have probably heard the old saying, "let your conscience be your guide"? Well, that's only if you have the right information stored in your conscience. Sometimes people are able to argue with their conscience and win. Still others can negotiate with their conscience and be just fine with going about in their folly. Then there are others who are just not informed and the conscience has nothing in it to combat temptation. You see if the conscience does an effective job of reserving the good stuff that has been processed by the intellect, then it enhances the function of the next part which is the will.

The intellect does its job and processes, the conscience stores data for later use, and the will is the part of the heart that gives the rest of the body permission to carry out the tasks. If you do anything, you willed to do it. You have probably heard the other saying, "where there is a will there is a way"? The will allows you to do whatever the conscience stores because the will normally carries out what the conscience will let it carry out. We often tell our children to think before you speak or act. To do this the intellect, conscience and will need to work in concert. If the process is correct then the storage should be safe and the will is free to work.

The last part of this heart is the emotion. This part of the heart is supposed to respond to what the will does. A young boy helps an elderly lady with her groceries. She thanks him and gives him some money for his troubles. When he goes away happy, it's the response of the emotional part. Now when we put everything together we have the information processed by the intellect, stored in the conscience, carried out by the will and responded to by the emotional section.

So now what if this model was flipped? This is the condition that exists more often than not. A person that has this model flipped processes everything through his or her emotions first. Then it is immediately carried out by the will and then the effects are lamented by the conscience. If that is not enough, the intellect then is the last to know and that's where the pity-party begins.

So, here is what this looks like in real time. A woman goes to a party and meets a nice-looking guy. He is charming and sweet and talked about puppies. They have a few drinks and before she knows it they are joined at the lips in passionate foreplay. The scenario seems perfect, he is saying all the right things and he is so gentle and it has been a while since a man has made her feel like this. She ends up going to a hotel with him and he's gone before she wakes up. There is a thank you note on the table with a Danish and coffee. She realizes that she does not even know his last name. No phone number, she is not sure where he works and there really is not a way for her to contact him. She finally says, "How did I end up in this predicament?" What happened is that she was totally processing the evening through her emotions. Feelings can be very irresistible when coupled with strong desire. Emotions can be a powerful tool in fueling our passion, but when it is misplaced as in this case, it can be devastating.

In the example, the woman was sincere in her thoughts, she just was not logical. The man was very logical as he was able to get exactly what he wanted. Impulsive decisions are normally emotional. So once anyone sees impulsiveness you are dealing with someone that is somewhat unstable. Emotions can never be used as a filter and it was never designed to be a filter. Once through the emotions, the will just responds and the conscience as stated is convicted. Sadly that does not take place until the morning after. She woke up with a convicted conscience and on her drive home her intellect assesses the damage and says, "How can I have been so stupid?"

This model spins on an axis so at any given time you can go from having your intellect on top to having it spun to the bottom. This model needs an anchor to keep it in place. Jesus is supposed to be our anchor which means that if we just followed the things that are in scripture, we should live better than the rest of the world.

Love proves the existence of God in the very soul of the believer. A child of God demonstrates to the rest of the world this character that is at the heart of our creator. Take us out of the world and there is no love. Dear reader, we need to understand that not only did God not give us the spirit of fear, but he did give us a sound mind (which should lead atop our model), power and of course love. Use it wisely my friend and make sure your top filter is intellect.

Chapter 7

I can forgive

Fear is a stronger opponent than we think. Sometimes it is not always the idea of being afraid of something, but sometimes fear hides pride and prejudice. When we go back in American history and understand the psychology of why we had to have a civil war, it was far more than just the economy at stake. This is so because, for the South, there would be an outcome that would affect generations to come. The "Good ole' Days" as they knew it were becoming extinct.

A life where southerners could proudly display their "footstools" in public and always present themselves higher than the people they were standing on. Free labor was considered the best economy because it literally was on the backs of someone else. And these southerners were willing to die to keep it that way.

Fast forward 50 years and change was still hard to come by. Sure there were new laws, but enforcement of those laws was far from consistent and things still were not equal. This is the period of our history where we were trying to give folks time to come around to the right idea and abandon those unfair, destructive beliefs.

Advance ahead 50 more years and we enter the 20th century and eventually a civil rights movement must take place for equality to be born. Remember we are still in a democracy where we pledge allegiance to a flag and we proclaim that in order to form a more perfect union, we established

justice and ensure domestic tranquility
– sounds beautiful doesn't it?
Fifty years later and on the outside we
look better than we did 100 years ago,
but there are more African-Americans
in prison now than were lynched and
in slavery. Are we really better off? A
society should be judged by its justice
system and our country lead the world
in prisoners per capita. Wealth in this
country is dispensed so unevenly that
one percent of those living here have
more wealth than the combined 99
percent left.

A long time ago a few group of men
decided what type of life you could
have, how far you could advance, what
you were going to eat, what kind of
medicine you would take and how
much education would be allowed. As
a result we are dying faster and sooner
than normal. We take far more "pills"
than the rest of the world and we live

in fear. Well, this explains why we need Jesus, but what does it say about forgiveness?

Forgiveness is an act practiced by those who are free. I am talking about the freedom that comes in Christ Jesus. More than just the saving of our souls, Jesus' gospel broke the bonds of sin and set us free. The Apostle Paul said that he "led captivity captive and gave gifts to men." Forgiveness is as much a part of being a Christian as crying is a part of being a baby. It's a characteristic of the new creature we become in Christ. A true child of God is not afraid to forgive. There is no fear of losing a position or status, there is no fear of shame or embarrassment or even becoming less than. Forgiveness is the understanding that God forgave me and my gratitude I give to God is to pay it forward.

America had a double shock after the church shooting in Charleston, SC where a young white male actually sat through a bible study before shooting and killing some of the parishioners of the church – this was the first shock. The second shock was hearing news reports that days after this horrible event the families had already forgiven the shooter. To the carnal eye these people were crazy, but to the spiritual eye these people looked like Christians. Forgiveness is something that only comes from our father in heaven. The world would be a better place with more people like these. Forgiveness is a battle, not against the person who needs forgiveness, but against our own flesh. When bad things happen to a Christian the incident kindles the war between the flesh and the spirit. We have a decision to make then...to honor God with our actions or give in to the flesh. The flesh will advise us to seek revenge. In the spirit we know that vengeance belongs to God so in essence what the carnal or flesh wants you to do is be a thief and take what belongs to God. When trouble comes, vengeance belongs to God and he gives us forgiveness expecting us to exercise our right to forgive. It's a choice that is made to glorify God despite the fear of losing something in the process.

The only reason I need to forgive is that God allowed me to taste it and gave me the ability to give that feeling of "forgiven" to someone else. I can forgive because God created me that way. He created me in Christ Jesus for this purpose so when I forgive, I become like my creator and this glorifies him.

There are people, Christians and non-Christians, living with bitterness because they will not forgive. These people are shortening their lives by holding grudges and wasting good memory on hating instead of loving. And to make matters worse, God promised to forgive the same way we do (Matt. 7:2; 18) so basically if I forgive, so will he forgive me. Conversely, if I choose to hold a grudge against someone then woe unto me on Judgment Day because I did not make my calling and election sure. The plan that God has for me includes forgiveness. And he gave me enough forgiveness for myself and anyone I come in contact with that needs it. Praises be to God for this wonderful gift.

Chapter 8

A life of meaningful service

We are a society of extremes – and it doesn't have to be that way. The way things are going we will of course destroy our planet and ourselves. There seems to be no middle ground that anyone wants to choose. Think about it? We live in a world where people actually starve to death. And then on the other side of the world there are people so obese that they struggle through their lives suffering from degenerative diseases until they die.

We have generations of people in poverty living in conditions that are deplorable and then just a few days journey away; there are people so wealthy that it would take four generations to spend it all. This crazy world has Christians who practice hate, record keeping of wrongdoing and feel murder can be justified, while there are atheist seeking to live in peace and harmony. There are workaholics who hold down two and three jobs at a time while others can't seem to find one job.

Watching these conditions make it difficult sometimes to see God. So many people have left organized religion because expectations were not met. People calling themselves Christians were there speaking things they ought not and were offensive, someone needed financial assistance and was sent away, the homeless could not find shelter and those who were hungry continued to starve. We know in our bibles that Jesus challenged his disciples with these very things and placed himself in these conditions and encouraged them for their service to him in these areas. They were confounded and asked Jesus when was he in such shape that they would have need to help him. This next part is so profound; he says if you have done it for anyone, you have done it for me.

The God that knows the hearts of mankind produces this scenario to challenge us all. Jesus said that when you help people it's just like you are helping me. Really Jesus? You are saying that the homeless guy that smells needs to be handled with the care I would give to the savior? Yep! You mean to tell me, Jesus that this person who won't get off his bum to help himself gets to benefit from my hard-earned money? Certainly! Clearly for us, our spirit is willing, but our flesh is so weak. But this is God's mandate and he did not make this an option, but a response to his goodness.

So because God has been so good to me, I want to help spread his goodness. And there are people who need to hear his goodness, but they have things in their way to distort the message. What Jesus called me to do in that story is clear the noise! Homelessness, hunger, and hard times are all distortions of my message. In other words, it is difficult to hear the goodness of the gospel through your hunger pains.

This does not mean that the Church is to be responsible for the welfare of the poor. It also doesn't mean that the congregation should open a soup kitchen or have quarterly clothing drives. These things are not bad, it's just they are not the function of the Lord's church. We spread the gospel. The service that we give to the

community has strings attached. We
are actually supposed to use the trials
of the poor as an opportunity to share
the goodness of God with its benefits.

The church is supposed to work like
a hospital, where sick people reside
and get well and the sick travel there
for healing. You would be hard
pressed to find a hospital today that
specializes in clothing drives. It would
be quite difficult to find a hospital that
feeds the homeless too. Why is this? It
is not because the hospital
administration could care less about
those suffering, it's because it is not
the function of the hospital to provide
such things.

The mission of the church is to seek
and save the lost. Then we take those
recently saved and teach them how to
live for Christ. The process gets
duplicated until finally we have

created a community of believers where faith, hope and love abide. We need to raise our conscience level higher so that we are more sensitive to our fellow man.

We are consciously aware of the spiritual warfare going on inside of us. The physical world that we live in is a manifestation of that war. The character of folks we meet are representations of this war. Sometimes feelings get hurt and God somehow gets blamed. Many have blamed this sinful world's problems on our loving father.

When we see the darkness of this world, it sometimes looks like we are losing the spiritual battle. We see sin reign, hatred in abundance an ego elevated beyond the heights of selfishness. Somehow we lost sight of God's plan. Here's the plan: God wanted to show his goodness to us so he gave us grace and mercy. We were to show our gratitude through imitation of his son and obedience. Studying God's word and living it are important to conforming to the image of his Son. I need to trust his word and follow it. To trust and obey his word I have to know it. His word is the only thing we have here on earth that will change the hearts of men.

The model he gave us to encourage us to fight this good fight of faith is the burning bush. When Moses saw the burning bush it instantly grabbed his attention. It was truly something to marvel. Moses was instantly drawn to this phenomenon and that is exactly where he met God.

If we are doing it correctly then we would be surrounded by the fires of this world, but never consumed. We would remain in this state until he sent his son back to get us. But more importantly we would have the same effect on the world that the burning bush had on Moses and the same effect would happen – the world would meet God and understand him better through this incredible model. This is our task.

Then Jesus comes back and would take us from the burning bush to a new tabernacle not made with hands. We would then dwell with him forever. But in the meantime we are to simply let our light shine bright in the midst of this dark world. We were never supposed to eliminate the darkness but create as much light as we could. The light would be in the forms of love, justice, forgiveness, service and goodness.

Despite the evils of this world, our God wants to see the flourishing beauty he created. He expects for this creation to not conform to the world, but be transformed by a renewed mind. This creation is precious to him. He called this creation Christians!

Epilogue

Wow, what a journey! I am honored to present this information of change to those who are seeking. This will not be received by everyone, but praises to the Father for his wisdom, grace and mercy.

It is my sincere hope that at this stage you are saying to yourself that there is much work to do. We have a lot of work to do in the area of applying these truths in our life. The truths presented here were designed to eliminate fear. To know that God presented a perfect system and imperfect people are trying to administer it.

We cannot blame God for our imperfections; we must regroup and make sure we are following *his* plan. I still get excited to know that I have been placed on a plan by my God that I cannot mess up! I am full of joy in understanding unconditional love as my greatest weapon and I need to apply it liberally in this life. I love because God first loved me. Also, I love the fact that I am not harboring ill feelings about anyone because I live forgiven therefore I forgive. And the service that I give is part of my honor to serve my king. I am glad to be a citizen of the kingdom despite the frustrations of others in the body, I am glad to serve. This is only the beginning. There are many other principles in the word of God that need a spotlight and I am happy to provide that light. Volume 2 in this series will also attempt to illuminate God's truths that we may do justly, and to love mercy and walk humbly with our God. To be continued . . .

www.ingramcontent.com/pod-product-compliance
Lightning Source LLC
LaVergne TN
LVHW021538080426
835509LV00019B/2711